INTERNATIONAL CENTRE FOR MECHANICAL SCIENCES

COURSES AND LECTURES - No. 138

GIUSEPPE LONGO
UNIVERSITY OF TRIESTE - ITALY

QUANTITATIVE - QUALITATIVE MEASURE OF INFORMATION

COURSE HELD AT THE DEPARTMENT
OF AUTOMATION AND INFORMATION
JUNE - JULY 1972

SPRINGER-VERLAG   WIEN GMBH 1972

This work is subject to copyright.

All rights are reserved,

whether the whole or part of the material is concerned

specifically those of translation, reprinting, re-use of illustrations,

broadcasting, reproduction by photocopying machine

or similar means, and storage in data banks.

© 1972 Springer-Verlag Wien

Originally published by Springer-Verlag Wien-New York 1972

ISBN 978-3-211-81182-5   ISBN 978-3-7091-2796-4 (eBook)
DOI 10.1007/978-3-7091-2796-4

PREFACE

These lecture notes cover most of the results obtained by several Authors in the attempt of completing Shannon's approach to Information Theory with some "qualitative" parameter, which we call here "utility".

It is not clear yet whether this attempt will turn out to be successful. Although from a mathematical point of view the results obtained so far are not very deep, it is quite possible that some applications will be found that can profit of this approach and justify it a posteriori.

I thank my audience for the patience and the interest exhibited during the course, as well as for the many stimulating discussions I had with them.

Udine, June 1972

Chapter 1

FUNDAMENTALS ABOUT CODING FOR NOISELESS CHANNELS

In this Chapter we wish to summarize some well-known results about variable-length encoding techniques for finite information Sources feeding noiseless Channels. This survey is not to be exhaustive, it is just to provide a foundation for subsequent developments.

The usual Shannon block-diagram for a transmission link (Fig. 1.1) will be constantly referred to, and the following illustration will

Fig. 1.1. Shannon's block diagram for a communication link.

provide notations and definitions.

The Source is any device able to output, one at each unit time, letters from its alphabet $\mathcal{A} = \{a_1, a_2, \ldots, a_k\}$ ($k \geq 2$). This letter generation is a random operation and therefore may provide information. The noiseless Channel is any device able to transfer symbols from its input to its output. The symbols transferred by the channel, $b_1, b_2, \ldots, b_m$ say, are in general different from the a_i's, which in turn cannot be dealt with by the channel.

It follows that if one wishes to transmit the (information carried by) the letters output by the source to the User, it is necessary to translate, or to encode, these letters, or sequences of these letters, by means of codewords, i.e. sequences of b_j's. This encoding, however, should permit a faithful recovering of the original letter sequences; in other words it should be uniquely decodable. The operations of encoding and decoding are accomplished by the two blocks marked encoder and decoder.

The simplest way of encoding is to associate a codeword $w(a_i)$ to each letter a_i and therefore the codeword $w(a_{i_1}, a_{i_2}, \ldots, a_{i_n})$ for a sequence $a_{i_1}, a_{i_2}, \ldots, a_{i_n}$ is just the juxtaposition of $w(a_{i_1}), w(a_{i_2}), \ldots, w(a_{i_n})$. These simple-letter codes are important of their own and moreover provide a basis for more general codes.

Since the channel is noiseless and therefore introduces no transmission error we are only concerned in minimizing transmission cost. One very elementary approach to this concept is to consider the transmission cost of a source letter a_i as proportional to the length $l(w(a_i))$ of its codeword, being the length of a sequence the number of symbols it contains. Therefore minimizing transmission cost amounts to minimizing the length of the transmitted codewords, more pre-

Unique Decipherability

cisely to minimizing the average length, being the source statistics the relevant one for averaging. Obviously this minimization should be carried out while keeping the property of unique decipherability, otherwise the problem would be trivially solved.

To be more precise let us give some definitions:

Definition 1.1

A simple letter code $\{w(a_1),\ldots,w(a_k)\}$ is uniquelly decipherable or decodable if there is no pair of different source sequences having the same code, i.e.

$$w(a_{i_1}, a_{i_2}, \ldots, a_{i_n}) = w(a_{j_1}, a_{j_2}, \ldots, a_{j_m})$$

implies $n = m$ and $i_k = j_k$, $1 \leq k \leq n$.

Definition 1.2

If $y_{i_1} \cdots y_{i_r} = u$ is any sequence of letters taken from any alphabet, then $y_{i_1} \cdots y_{i_s} = v$ $(s \leq r)$ is a segment of u. The empty sequence (having no letter) is a segment of every sequence.

Definition 1.3

A simple letter code is a prefix code if no $w(a_i)$ is a segment of another $w(a_j)$ (for $i \neq j$).

These definitions allow us to state the following

Lemma 1.1

A simple letter prefix code is uniquely decodable.

The proof of the lemma is trivial.

The importance of uniquely decodable codes prompt us to look for conditions on their existence. The main result in this direction is the following

Theorem 1.1

Let $l_1, l_2, \ldots, l_k$ be the lengths of a simple letter code for the alphabet $\mathcal{A} = \{a_1, a_2, \ldots, a_k\}$ built up by means of an alphabet $\mathcal{B}$ of size m. The code can be uniquely decodable only if the so-called Kraft inequality is satisfied:

$$(1.1) \qquad \sum_{i=1}^{n} m^{-l_i} \leq 1 .$$

Moreover, if (1.1) holds, then a prefix (hence uniquely decodable) simple letter code exists with lengths $l_1, l_2, \ldots, l_k$.

There are several proofs for Theorem 1.1 which can be found in any standard text-book of Information Theory (see e.g. Gallager (1968) or Katona (1970)) and since our main concern is not directed to this point, the reader is referred to the literature.

We have already mentioned in an informal way that the relevant problem in noiseless channel coding is the minimization of the "average" length of the codewords. We wish now to give a more precise meaning to this concept. If the finite source we are considering is memoryless, i.e. if it outputs the subsequent letters independently and according to the same probability distribution, say

$$\mathcal{P} = \{p_1, p_2, \ldots, p_k\} \quad (p_i > 0, \sum_1^k p_i = 1) \tag{1.2}$$

then obviously a sound definition for the average codeword length is

$$L = \sum_1^k p_i l_i \tag{1.3}$$

where l_i is the length of $w(a_i)$.

The memoryless source, however, is a very particular sort of source. A definition for the average code length when a non-memoryless source is given can be the following. Considering the source as a random process

$$\Xi = \xi(1), \xi(2), \ldots, \xi(n) \tag{1.4}$$

where each of the random variables $\xi(n)$ takes on values from the finite alphabet $\mathcal{A}$, the random variable " length of the codeword for the n first source letters" is defined in a natural way as follows:

$$L_n = \text{length of } w(\xi(1), \xi(2), \ldots, \xi(n)) \tag{1.5}$$

Then the following definition is adopted:

<u>Definition 1.4</u>

The quantity L is the average codeword length of the code considered if

(1.6) $$\lim_{n \to \infty} \text{prob} \frac{L_n}{n} = L$$

In other words L is the average codeword length if for any fixed $\varepsilon > 0$ one has

(1.7) $$\text{Prob}\left(\left|\frac{L_n}{n} - L\right| > \varepsilon\right) < \delta(n, \varepsilon)$$

and

(1.8) $$\lim_{n \to \infty} \delta(n, \varepsilon) = 0 \; .$$

It is to be remarked that the probability measure involved in (1.6) and (1.7) is one attached to the information source considered. We only mention that if the random process Ξ is stationary and ergodic, then the average codeword length exists.

It is well known that in the case of a finite memoryless source $\mathcal{J}$, specified by

(1.9) $$\mathcal{J} = \begin{pmatrix} a_1 & a_2 & \ldots & a_k \\ p_1 & p_2 & \ldots & p_k \end{pmatrix} = \begin{pmatrix} \mathcal{A} \\ \mathcal{P} \end{pmatrix}$$

the Shannon entropy

(1.10) $$H(\mathcal{J}) = H(\mathcal{P}) \triangleq - \sum_{i}^{k} p_i \log p_i$$

plays a fundamental role. We do not wish to describe here the well-known properties of $H(\mathcal{P})$, we only mention its relevance to the problem of noiseless coding. Actually the following is true:

Theorem 1.2

Each uniquely decodable simple-letter code for a memoryless source as in (1.9) has an average length $L = \sum_{1}^{k} p_i l_i$ satisfying

$$L \geq \frac{H(\mathcal{P})}{\log m} \quad (*) \tag{1.11}$$

Proof

We start from the nonnegative character of the I-divergence $I(\mathcal{P} \| \mathcal{Q})$ between any two probability distributions $\mathcal{P}$ and $\mathcal{Q}$ over the same finite set:

$$I(\mathcal{P} \| \mathcal{Q}) \triangleq \sum_{1}^{k} p_i \log \frac{p_i}{q_i} \geq 0 \tag{1.12}$$

and specialize $\mathcal{P}$ and $\mathcal{Q}$ as follows: let $\mathcal{P}$ be the source probability distribution given in (1.9) and $\mathcal{Q} = \{q_i\}_{i=1}^{k}$ be defined by

$$q_i = \frac{m^{-l_i}}{\sum_{j=1}^{k} m^{-l_j}} \quad (1 \leq i \leq k) \tag{1.13}$$

(*) Unless differently stated, logarithms are always taken to the base 2.

Now (1.12) yields

$$0 \le \sum_{i}^{k} p_i \log p_i m^{l_i} \left(\sum_{j}^{k} m^{-l_j} \right) = -H(\mathcal{P}) + \left(\sum_{i}^{k} l_i p_i \right) \log m +$$

$$+ \log \left(\sum_{i}^{k} m^{-h_i} \right)$$

and, since by the Kraft inequality which must hold, $\log \left(\sum_{i}^{k} m^{-h_i} \right) \le 0$ also

$$H(\mathcal{P}) \le \log m \, L$$

whence the thesis (1.11).

Q.d.e.

One can wonder how tight the lower bound given by Theorem 1.2 is. The answer lies in the condition of vanishing for the I-divergence, which is $p_i = q_i$ ($1 \le i \le k$). Since m and the p_i's are given and since the l_i should be integers, the condition $p_i = m^{-l_i}$ cannot be satisfied in general. The best one can do is to choose the lengths l_i in such a way that

(1.14) $\qquad m^{-l_i} \le p_i < m^{-l_i+1} \qquad (1 \le i \le k)$

which is obviously always possible. If one adopts this choice, then the result expressed by the following theorem holds:

Theorem 1.3

The finite memoryless source $\mathcal{S}$ in (1.9) admits a

An Upper Bound on L

uniquely decodable single-letter code whose average length $L = \sum_{i=1}^{k} p_i l_i$ satisfies

$$\frac{H(\mathcal{P})}{\log m} \leq L < \frac{H(\mathcal{P})}{\log m} + 1 \qquad (1.15)$$

Proof.

Starting from (1.14), taking logarithms, multiplying by p_i and summing over i from 1 to k we get

$$\log m \sum_{i=1}^{k} p_i l_i \geq H(\mathcal{P}) > \log m \sum_{i=1}^{k} p_i l_i - \log m$$

whence the result (1.15) follows immediately.

Q.d.e.

The memoryless character of the source immediately suggests to adopt a block encoding technique for improving things, i.e. for lowering the average length. This improvement is made possible by the additive property of entropy for independent schemes: if $\mathcal{S}^n$ is the n-th extension of the given memoryless source, then its entropy $H(\mathcal{P}^n)$ equals $nH(\mathcal{P})$. Now applying Theorem 1.3 above to the finite memoryless source $\mathcal{S}^n$ gives.

Theorem 1.4 The memoryless n-th extension $\mathcal{S}^n$ of the finite source $\mathcal{S}$ in (1.9) admits a uniquely decodable block code whose average length $L^{(n)} \triangleq \sum_{u \in \mathcal{A}^n} \mathcal{P}(u) l(w(u))$ satisfies

$$\frac{nH(\mathcal{P})}{\log m} \leq L^{(n)} < \frac{nH(\mathcal{P})}{\log m} + 1 \quad . \qquad (1.16)$$

Proof.

It is the same as for Theorem 1.3, where only condition (1.14) is replaced by

$$(1.17) \qquad m^{-l(w(u))} \leq \mathcal{P}(u) < m^{-l(w(u))+1} \qquad \text{all} \quad u \in \mathcal{R}^n$$

and the sums are taken over all n-sequences of elements from $\mathcal{R}$.

Q.d.e.

An important consequence is the following

Corollary 1.1

The finite memoryless source $\mathcal{J}$ in (1.9) admits a uniquely decodable block code whose average length per source letter, $L^{(n)}/n$, is as close to $H(\mathcal{P})/\log m$ as we wish provided only n is large enough.

Proof

Divide everywhere by n in (1.16) and pass to the limit as n goes to ∞.

Q.d.e.

To close this chapter we wish to linger a bit on the so-called " principle of conservation of entropy" [Katona and Tusnády (1967), Csiszár, Katona, Tusnády (1969), Katona (1970)]. We can roughly summarize the above results on on the average length for a uniquely decipherable single-letter code for a finite memoryless source by saying that at one's best one gets

Entropy per Symbol

$$\min L \cong \frac{H(\mathcal{P})}{\log m} . \qquad (1.18)$$

After the encoding procedure, at the output end of the encoder, one gets a new random process, which can be considered as another information source, say

$$\Theta = \vartheta(1), \vartheta(2), \ldots, \vartheta(n) \qquad (1.19)$$

whose character, however, is not necessarily memoryless, or even stationary, if the input process is memoryless. This raises the problem of defining what the average information content of a code letter is, in other words of defining the entropy of an arbitrary discrete random process. If $\xi(i,j)$ stands for $(\xi(i), \xi(i+1), \ldots, \xi(j))$ $(i \leq j)$ and $P(\xi(1,j) = u)$ for $\text{Prob}(\xi(1) = a_{i_1}, \xi(2) = a_{i_2}, \ldots, \xi(j) = a_{i_j})$ where $u = a_{i_1}, a_{i_2}, \ldots, a_{i_j}$ then the entropy of the n first letters is defined as

$$H(\xi(1,n)) = -\sum_{u \in \mathcal{A}^n} P(\xi(1,n) = u) \log P(\xi(1,n) = u) \qquad (1.20)$$

and the entropy per symbol of the process considered, or of the corresponding information source, is defined as

$$H(\Xi) = \lim_{n \to \infty} \frac{H(\xi(1,n))}{n} \qquad (1.21)$$

if the limit exists (*).

Since we already defined what is the average code length, see definition 1.4, we are now in a position to give a precise formulation of the principle of conservation of entropy.

Theorem 1.5

Let $\mathcal{S}$ be an information source and $\mathcal{W}$ a uniquely decodable simple-letter code for $\mathcal{S}$ using an alphabet of size m If the entropy $H(\mathcal{S})$ of $\mathcal{S}$ exists and if the average code length L exists and $L > 0$, then

$\alpha)$ $H(\Theta)$ exists

$\beta)$ $H(\Theta) = \dfrac{H(\mathcal{S})}{L}$

where $H(\Theta)$ is the entropy, as defined by (1.21), of the random process Θ generated by the code acting on the source $\mathcal{S}$.

For a proof of this result, see Katona (1970), p. 33 and following.

It is now easy to see that Theorem 1.2 is an immediate consequence of thesis $\beta)$ of Theorem 1.5, since in any case when there exists the entropy $H(\Theta)$ of the random process then

$$H(\Theta) \leq \log m$$

(*) The limit in (1.21) exists e.g. if the source Ξ is stationary. For a proof see e.g. Katona (1970) p. 30.

and therefore from $H(\Theta) = \frac{H(\mathcal{J})}{\log m}$ inequality (1.11) follows, since $H(\mathcal{J}) = H(\mathcal{S})$ in the memoryless case.

Chapter 2

THE COMMUNICATION PROBLEM : THE STATISTICAL, THE SEMANTIC AND THE EFFECTIVENESS VIEWPOINTS − SOURCES HAVING UTILITIES AND THE USEFUL ENTROPY

In this Chapter we intend to give a general motivation for the subsequent developments. Although a mathematical treatment needs no motivation in general, but only sound definitions and tools, it seems however that the particular topic treated requires further and deeper foundations. Actually its relevance to practical, i.e. non-mathematical, fields makes it hard to conceive information theory per se; this isolative view could have two kinds of negative effects. On one hand one could develop formal theories (e.g. axiomatic approaches or the like) having really no relationship with communication problems or the like, and call them nonetheless " information theory" plus some additional qualifications; on the other hand, even worse, one could loose view of the origins of the theory and try to apply it to specific problems for which the theory yields completely mistaken or meaningless solutions. What is really important is to be aware of the intrinsic limitations of Information Theory, to avoid improper applications while trying to enlarge its structure and scope on the basis of solid and specific motivations.

It is generally aknowledged that one important reason for the success of Shannon's approach to Information Theory is the exceeding simplicity of his models for source and channel. We shall be concerned mainly with the information source. The simplification lies in that the task of the communication link is merely to reproduce a copy of the source output in such a way that it may be distinguished from any other possible output; therefore the description of the source is limited to a list of its possible outputs, without any attention paid to their meaning or effect on an observer whatsoever.

This corresponds to what Weaver has called " Level A" of communication problems (see Shannon & Weaver (1949), p. 24) - Weaver's level A is concerned with the question " How accurately can the symbols of communication be transmitted?"

Obviously, once these symbols are clearly and unambigously distinguishable, nothing is implied as to the meaning they convey relative to the meaning they should convey according to the source wishes. This remark leads to Weaver's " Level B" of communication problems, dealing with the question " How precisely do the transmitted symbols convey the desired meaning?" Again a further level is conceivable, reflecting the distinction between actual and potential information. The third level, level C, which Weaver characterizes by means of the question " How effectively does the received meaning effect conduct in the desired way?", clearly differs from the semantic one, although it rests on it. The cybernetic character of level C , conveyed by the words " affect conduct" , in its behavioural definiteness is much easier to deal with than level B , since semantic questions are always rather thorny.

In what follows we shall be concerned with the interrelationships between level A and level C . We shall illustrate what can be done, and has been done, in the direction of a formalization of this problem. All this of course will rest upon rough simplifications, of the same type of Shannon's; whether these amputations are tolerable is questionable, and only the results the theory will lead to, can answer the question.

The first remark for completing the scheme (1.9) of an information source with some parameters dealing with effectiveness, is that this completion should reflect a subjective character which is lacking in Shannon's setup where only statistics is present. We do not intend to plounge into such problems as whether probability has an objective or subjective character; we only remark that in practical cases the source statistics (or the statistical structure of any random experiment) is derived from repetition of trials, while the subjective parameters we intend to introduce have in general nothing to do with probability or statistics.

As Belis and Guiașu (1968) have remarked, any outcome of a random experience, apart from its probability has some "utility" or "value" for the observer, relative to some specified goal. Thus they proposed to measure this utility aspect of the outcome by means of a "utility distribution" $\mathcal{U} = \{u_1, u_2, \ldots, u_k\}$, where each of the u_i is a nonnegative real number accounting for the utility, or value, of the i-th outcome for the given pair observer-goal. As a consequence, the scheme of a finite random experiment, instead of (1.9), takes on the following form:

$$(2.1) \qquad \mathcal{S} = \begin{pmatrix} a_1 & a_2 & \ldots & a_k \\ p_1 & p_2 & \ldots & p_k \\ u_1 & u_2 & \ldots & u_k \end{pmatrix} = \begin{pmatrix} \mathcal{A} \\ \mathcal{P} \\ \mathcal{U} \end{pmatrix}$$

which of course can represent also an information source whose letters have a definite value for the receiver. The utility distribution $\mathcal{U}$, as we say, in general is independent from the probability distribution $\mathcal{P}$, and one can easily conceive random experiments having the same statistical distribution but very different utility distributions as being basically different as fas as the observer is concerned.

The occurrence of a particular outcome a_i brings to the observer a quantity of information measured by its self-information $I(p_i) = -\log p_i$. The problem is to construct an analogous function measuring the quantity of "useful information"

Axioms for the Useful Self-Information

brought by the occurrence of a_i having probability p_i and utility u_i. This "useful self-information" function $I(p_i, u_i)$ may be chosen as to satisfy the following two postulates (due to Belis and Guiaşu):

1) If all the events (simple and compound) of the random experience have the same utility, $u > 0$ say, then the useful self-information provided by the logical product $a_1 \wedge a_2$ of two statistically independent events a_1 and a_2 is the sum of the useful self-informations provided by a_1 and a_2 :

$$I(p_1 p_2, u) = I(p_1, u) + I(p_2, u) \qquad (2.2)$$

where $p_1 p_2$ is the probability of $a_1 \wedge a_2$, for any p_1 and p_2.

2) The useful self-information provided by outcome a_i is proportional to its utility u_i i.e. for each nonnegative λ the following holds

$$I(p_i, \lambda u_i) = \lambda I(p_i, u_i) \qquad (2.3)$$

These two postulates are sufficient to determine the form of the useful self-information $I(p, u)$ of an event; more precisely

Theorem 2.1 (Belis - Guiaşu)

If $I = I(p, u)$ is a continuous function of p and u ($0 \leq p \leq 1$, $u \geq 0$) satisfying postulates 1) and 2) above, then

(2.4) $\quad I = I(u,p) = -ku\log p$

where k is an arbitrary positive constant.

Proof.

Let $u_i = 1$ and $\lambda = u$ in (2.3), so

(2.5) $\quad I(p_i, u) = u I(p_i, 1)$

let now $u = 1$ in (2.2), so

(2.6) $\quad I(p_1 p_2, 1) = I(p_1, 1) + I(p_2, 1)$

Since $I(p,1)$ depends only on p, or equivalently on $\log p$ we have $I(p,1) = F(\log p)$ and therefore from (2.6)

$$F(\log p_1 p_2) = F(\log p_1) + F(\log p_2)$$

and setting $x = \log p_1$, $y = \log p_2$, also

$$F(x+y) = F(x) + F(y).$$

This functional equation has only one continuous solution, i.e. $F(x) = ax$ being a an arbitrary constant. Going backwards we get

$$I(u,p) = -ku\log p$$

being k a positive constant if we wish to have a nonnegative information function. Q.d.e.

The Useful Entropy

The mean value of the useful self-information (2.4) with respect to the probability distribution $\mathcal{P}$, i.e.

$$H(\mathcal{P}, \mathcal{U}) = -k \sum_{1}^{u} p_i u_i \log p_i \qquad (2.7)$$

is obviously called the "useful entropy" of the random experiment (2.1) or of the random information source.

We emphasize some of the properties of $H(\mathcal{P}, \mathcal{U})$.

If the utilities of the various events are all equal, then $H(\mathcal{P}, \mathcal{U})$ reduces to the Shannon's entropy $H(\mathcal{P})$, apart from a multiplicative constant:

$$\text{If } u_i = \text{cost.} = u \qquad H(\mathcal{P}, \mathcal{U}) = -k \sum_{1}^{k} p_i \log p_i .$$

The useful entropy $H(\mathcal{P}, \mathcal{U})$ vanishes in three cases:

i) when the $\mathcal{P}$ distribution is degenerate

ii) when the utilities are all zero

iii) when, for non degenerate $\mathcal{P}$, $p_i > 0$ implies $u_i = 0$ and $u_j > 0$ implies $p_j = 0$.

Case iii) corresponds to a random experiment whose possible outcomes are useless and whose useful outcomes are impossible.

Let us also remark that the nonnegative character of the utilities may give an incomplete picture of some experiment where utilities are involved; actually one can conceive outcomes representing a drawback rather an advantage or an indifference for the observer relative to his goal. In other words, it seems that a utility measure should exhibit a relative character, rather a nonnegative one, but the theory developed so far deals only with nonnegative utilities.

Another remark deals with the monotonicity postulate 2). Actually there is no reason why we should choose such a particular monotonicity law as expressed by postulate 2); any increasing function $f(u)$ of the utility would do. In the case we choose an arbitrary (continuous) increasing function $f(u)$, the form of the useful entropy would be the following:

(2.8) $$H(\mathcal{P}, \mathcal{U}) = -k \sum_{i}^{u} p_i f(u_i) \log p_i$$

The useful entropy (2.7) corresponds to the choice $f(u_i) = u_i$.

Along with the elementary events a_i ($1 \le i \le k$) of the random experiment, we should also consider compound events, and it is necessary to assign a composition law for the utility of these events. Consider e.g. the logical union $a_i \vee a_j$ of two incompatible simple events, a_i and a_j. If we choose (Guiaşu (1971)) the following composition law:

(2.9) $$u(a_i \vee a_j) = \frac{u_i p_i + u_j p_j}{p_i + p_j}$$

with self-evident notations, then the property expressed by the following theorem is true:

Theorem 2.2 (Guiaşu)

Put $H_k(p_1, p_2, \ldots, p_k ; u_1, u_2, \ldots, u_k)$ instead

Properties of $H(\mathcal{P}, \mathcal{U})$

of $H(\mathcal{P}, \mathcal{U})$; if the composition law (2.9) holds, then

$$H_{k+1}(p_1, p_2, \ldots, p_{k-1}, p', p''; u_1, u_2, \ldots, u_{k-1}, u', u'') =$$

$$= H_k(p_1, p_2, \ldots, p_k; u_1, u_2, \ldots, u_k) + p_k H_2\left(\frac{p'}{p_k}, \frac{p''}{p_k}; u', u''\right)$$

(2.10)

where

$$p_k = p' + p'', \qquad u_k = \frac{u'p' + u''p''}{p' + p''} \qquad (2.11)$$

Proof

Write successively (letting the constant k be equal to 1):

$$H_{k+1}(p_1, p_2, \ldots, p_{k-1}, p', p''; u_1, u_2, \ldots, u_{k-1}, u', u'') =$$

$$= -\sum_{1}^{k-1} u_i p_i \log p_i - u'p' \log p' - u''p'' \log p'' =$$

$$= -\sum_{1}^{k-1} u_i p_i \log p_i - u_k p_k \log p_k + u_k p_k \log p_k - u'p' \log p' - u''p'' \log p'' =$$

$$= H_k(p_1, p_2, \ldots, p_k; u_1, u_2, \ldots, u_k) + (u'p' + u''p'') \log p_k - u'p' \log p' +$$

$$- u''p'' \log p'' =$$

$$= H_k(p_1, p_2, \ldots, p_k; u_1, u_2, \ldots, u_k) + p_k\left(-u'\frac{p'}{p_k} \log \frac{p'}{p_k} - u''\frac{p''}{p_k} \log \frac{p''}{p_k}\right) =$$

$$= H_k(p_1, p_2, \ldots, p_k; u_1, u_2, \ldots, u_k) + p_k H_2\left(\frac{p'}{p_k}, \frac{p''}{p_k}; u', u''\right).$$

Observe that Theorem 2.2 actually expresses a kind of "branching property" for the useful entropy, which is very close to the analogous property of Shannon's entropy. More than that, in case the utilities are all equal, the branching property of the useful entropy reduces to the branching property of Shannon's entropy, namely

$$H_{k+1}(p_1, p_2, \ldots, p_{k-1}, p', p'') =$$

$$= H_k(p_1, \ldots, p_{k-1}, p_k) + p_k H_2\left(\frac{p'}{p_k}, \frac{p''}{p_k}\right)$$

where $p_k = p' + p''$.

It is perhaps worthwhile mentioning one particular assignement for the utilities u_i, given by the following instance. (We remark explicitly that the formula (2.7) for the useful entropy can either been interpreted as a mean value of the random variable $-u_i \log p_i$ or as a weighted entropy, the weights being the utilities.)

Assume an observer is performing some random experiment whose outcomes $a_1, a_2, \ldots, a_k$ have the definite probability distribution $Q = \{q_1, q_2, \ldots, q_k\}$ which, on the other hand the observer does not know. Instead the observer has its own assessment as to the probability distribution of the experiment, say $P = \{p_1, p_2, \ldots, p_x\}$, which in general will be different from Q. Now if we ascribe to every outcome a_i a subjective weight

Coding Problems

$u_i = \frac{q_i}{p_i}$ $(1 \leq i \leq k)$, the corresponding useful entropy, will be

$$H_k\left(p_1,\ldots,p_k; \frac{q_1}{p_1},\ldots,\frac{q_k}{p_k}\right) = -\sum_1^k q_i \log p_i \qquad (2.12)$$

and, by virtue of inequality $\sum q_i \log \frac{q_i}{p_i} \geq 0$, the useful information (2.12) will be greater than the actual entropy $-\sum_1^k q_i \log q_i$ of the random experiment:

$$H\left(p_1,\ldots,p_k; \frac{q_1}{p_1},\ldots,\frac{q_k}{p_k}\right) \geq H(q_1,\ldots,q_k) \qquad (2.13)$$

the equality sign holding when $\mathcal{P} \equiv \mathcal{Q}$. Inequality (2.13) has the interesting interpretation that the incomplete knowledge of the probability distribution of a random experiment can only increase the average uncertainty before any performance of the random experiments.

Chapter 3

SOME CODING PROBLEMS AND THEOREMS RELATIVE TO SOURCES HAVING A UTILITY DISTRIBUTION

It is generally felt that in Information Theory some quantities become possibly of interest on account of some coding theorem in which they arise in a natural way. So for instance Shannon's entropy, although perhaps interesting on its own, becomes exceedingly important because of the existence of some deep theorems in which it plays a central role.

In this Chapter we wish to illustrate the coding-type results which are known so far relative to the useful entropy function $H(\mathcal{P}, \mathcal{U})$ introduced in Chapter Two. First of all we should make clear what the analogous of the average codeword length is when dealing with sources having utilities. If the right interpretation for the average length is that it is a sort of average cost, then we should look here for such an average cost, as well. Now to find out what the right interpretation would be, consider the following model of the transmission process: a memoryless source $\mathcal{S}$ having a utility distribution sends single letters from a finite alphabet through a noiseless channel, after suitable single-letter encoding. After receiving a letter, the user must pay an amount of money, which in general depends both on the utility the User associates to that letter and on the amount of work required for transmitting it. If we measure the latter by the length of the code word associated to the letter, then the cost c_i of receiveng the letter a_i is a function of u_i and of l_i, where we use the notations introduced in the previous Chapters:

(3.1) $$c_i = c_i(u_i, l_i) .$$

Figure 3.1 illustrates the transmission scheme

Minimizing the Transmission Cost

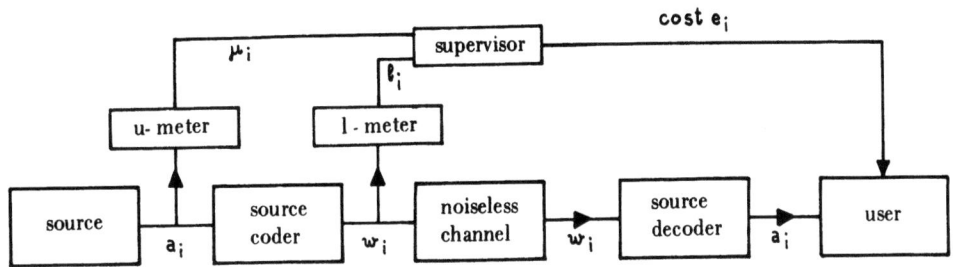

Fig. 3.1. Transmission scheme with utilities

It is important to remark that the utility w_i are assessed by the User, while the cost function is chosen by the Supervisor (*).

Now a good strategy for the User seems to be that of minimizing the average cost of information reception, i.e.:

$$\sum_1^k p_i c_i(u_i, l_i) \qquad (3.2)$$

Now the choice the Supervisor operates for the cost function $c_i(u_i, l_i)$ influences User's strategy in minimizing the quantity (3.2). E.g. a choice could be the following:

$$c_i(u_i, l_i) = u_i l_i \qquad (3.3)$$

and then the quantity to be minimized is

$$\sum_1^k p_i u_i l_i$$

(*) Remark that the Supervisor has no personal of metaphysical character; it is only a global way of indicating the counterpart of the User; e.g. Nature is a supervisor, or the particular character of a communication link is.

or equivalently the following

(3.4) $$L_u = \frac{\sum_i^k p_i u_i l_i}{\sum_i p_i u_i}$$

The quantity L_u appearing in (3.4) seems now to be the appropriate average cost function we were looking for; such a quantity is already known in the literature as the " average useful length" (Guiașu - Picard (1970)), but the present interpretation of it seems to be original. There are alternative interpretations:e.g. one could consider the amount of money to be paid for receiving a letter a_i to be a function of transmission burden (as measured by l_i) and some " storage" burden (measured by u_i) which depends on some structure or complexity of the actual representation of letter a_i. Also in this interpretation what the User should aim at is a reduction of the average cost as expressed by (3.4). Both these interpretations, as we shall see, can be extended to the case of block-encoding. Here is another interpretation which cannot be extended to the case of block-encoding, but is nevertheless worth mentioning.

Assume a large and complex machine undergoes occasional failures; let $\{a_1, a_2, \ldots, a_k\}$ be the possible failures and let p_i be the probability of failure a_i. Since not every break-down has the same importance as to the working capabilities of the machine, it seems appropriate to assign a " seriousness coefficient" μ_i to each failure a_i. Now assume

An Example

each failure a_i can be repaired in a time n_i which a priori is independent of the gravity of the failure itself. Consequently, when failure a_i occurs, the machine stops working at an extent u_i for a time n_i; and so the average work loss due to this family of possible break-downs is given by $\Sigma\, p_i\, u_i\, n_i$, which can be normalized and put in the form of an average useful length. It is not possible to find a good interpretation for the average cost of a sequence of failures, because this requires the definition of the corresponding loss and repairing time, which are not uniquely defined concepts. One should remark that this sort of considerations (i.e. the statistics and the gravity and repairing time of the possible break-downs) could perhaps help design the machine, leading to a better positioning of the elements for which a failure is more probable and/or more serious, so as to let their reparation be easier.

As we mentioned before, the choice $c_i(u_i, l_i) = n_i\, l_i$ is only one possibility, and one could have thought of the following choice:

$$c(u_i, l_i) = l_i\, 2^{n_i}. \qquad (3.2)$$

This choice leads to some very easy consequences, while the choice in (3.3) leads to something more complicated and surprising, which we shall illustrate in the sequel.

Now let us remark that the average useful length L_u can also be put in the following form

$$\text{(3.6)} \qquad L_u = \sum_{1}^{k} \frac{p_i u_i}{\sum_{j}^{k} p_j u_j} l_i = \sum_{1}^{k} q_i l_i$$

where the q_i'S defined by

$$\text{(3.7)} \qquad q_i = \frac{p_i u_i}{\sum_{j}^{k} p_j u_j}$$

form an auxiliary probability distribution Q. From (3.6) it is apparent that L_u is actually an average length, in the classical sense, however with respect to the new p.d. Q and not to the original p.d. $\mathcal{P} = \{p_1, p_2, \ldots, p_k\}$. This could give the impression that the classical theory applies also when utilities are involved, and that nothing new comes out. This is only partially true, and now we shall see the details.

The following theorems sets a lower bound on L_u for any uniquely decipherable code (in particular for any prefix code):

Theorem 3.1

Consider a simple letter code for the source of (2.1) and let its lengths $l_1, l_2, \ldots, l_k$ satisfy the Kraft inequality (1.1) $\sum_{1}^{k} m^{-l_i} \leq 1$. Then the average useful length defined by (3.4) satisfies the following inequality

$$\text{(3.8)} \qquad L_u \geq \frac{H(\mathcal{P}, \mathcal{U}) - \overline{u \log u} + \bar{u} \log \bar{u}}{\bar{u} \log m}$$

where $H(\mathcal{P}, \mathcal{U}) = -\sum_{1}^{k} p_i u_i \log p_i$ is the average useful information defined in Chapter 2, $\bar{u}$ is $\sum_{1}^{k} p_i u_i$ and $\overline{u \log u}$ is $\sum_{1}^{k} p_i u_i \log u_i$.

Proof

It is an immediate consequence of Theorem 1.2. Actually consider the p.d. Q instead of $\mathcal{P}$, according to (3.6); then Theorem 1.2 yields $L_u \geq \dfrac{H(Q)}{\log m}$, whence (3.8) follows since

$$H(Q) = \frac{H(\mathcal{P},\mathcal{U}) - \overline{u \log u} + \overline{u} \log \overline{u}}{\overline{u}} \quad . \tag{3.9}$$

Q.d.e.

One should remark that since $x \log x$ is a convex $\cup$ function the average $\overline{u \log u}$ is always greater than or equal to the quantity $\overline{u} \log \overline{u}$, and therefore the numerator in the lower bound of (3.8) can be strictly smaller than $H(\mathcal{P},\mathcal{U})$. One could wonder how tight this lower bound is, and an answer is given by the following theorem, still derived from the classical theory:

Theorem 3.2

By properly choosing the lengths $l_1, l_2, \ldots, l_k$ of the u.d. (*) simple-letter code, its average useful length can be made smaller than

$$\frac{H(\mathcal{P},\mathcal{U}) - \overline{u \log u} + \overline{u} \log \overline{u}}{\overline{u} \log m} + 1 \quad . \tag{3.10}$$

Proof.

Consider the auxiliary p.d. $Q = \{q\}_{i=1}^{k}$ and choose the lengths l_i as to satisfy

---

(*) The abbreviation u.d. will occasionally stand for uniquely decipherable.

(3.11) $$m^{-l_i} \le q_i \triangleq \frac{u_i p_i}{\bar{u}} < m^{-l_i+1} \quad (1 \le i \le k)$$

Now manipulating as in Theorem 1.3 the following inequalities are obtained

(3.12) $$\frac{H(Q)}{\log m} \le L_u < \frac{H(Q)}{\log m} + 1$$

The left-hand inequality is once more (3.8), while the right-hand one provides the desired upper bound on account of the expression (3.9) for $H(Q)$.

Q.d.e.

Now the user could feel it appropriate to ask for block encoding instead of single-letter encoding, and this to decrease the average useful length (i.e. average cost) per source letter. We wish to investigate now whether block encoding can really offer a better alternative.

The set-up is the usual one. An information source having a utility distribution outputs a sequence of letters, this sequence is subdivided into subblocks of length n which are encoded by means of the code alphabet. We assume the source is memoryless, and letting $\underline{v}^{(n)}$ or simply $\underline{v}$ be any n-length subblock, we consider the following quantities:

(3.13) $\mathcal{P}(\underline{v})$ = the probability of subblock $\underline{v}$

Block Encoding

$$\mathcal{U}(\underline{v}) = \quad \text{the utility of subblock } \underline{v} \quad (3.14)$$

$$\mathcal{N}(\underline{v}) = \quad \text{the length of the codeword for subblock } \underline{v}. \quad (3.15)$$

While $\mathcal{P}(\underline{v})$ is the product of the probabilities of the single letters of $\underline{v}$, on account of the memoryless character of the source, and $\mathcal{N}(\underline{v})$ depends of course on the code one adopts, there is no definition available for $\mathcal{U}(\underline{v})$. Of course we are at a great freedom as to the choice of $\mathcal{U}(\underline{v})$ but is it felt that a sound definition is the additive one:

$$\mathcal{U}(\underline{v}) = \sum_{j=1}^{n} u_{v_j} \quad \text{if} \quad \underline{v} = a_{i_1} a_{i_2} \ldots a_{i_n}. \quad (3.16)$$

Of course if the source were not memoryless, definition (3.16) should be properly modified. Now we are in a position to define the n-th order useful entropy $H^{(n)}(\mathcal{P}, \mathcal{U})$:

$$H^{(n)}(\mathcal{P}, \mathcal{U}) = - \sum_{\underline{v} \in \mathcal{A}^n} \mathcal{P}(\underline{v}) \mathcal{U}(\underline{v}) \log \mathcal{P}(\underline{v}), \quad (3.17)$$

where the sum is performed over all n-length sequences (all elements of $\mathcal{A}^n$); and the n-th order average useful length

$$L_u^{(n)} = \frac{\sum_{\underline{v} \in \mathcal{A}^n} \mathcal{N}(\underline{v}) \mathcal{P}(\underline{v}) \mathcal{U}(\underline{v})}{\sum_{\underline{v} \in \mathcal{A}^n} \mathcal{P}(\underline{v}) \mathcal{U}(\underline{v})}, \quad (3.18)$$

where the denominator of course can be considered as the n-th order average utility:

$$(3.19) \qquad \bar{u}^{(n)} = \sum_{\underline{v} \in \mathcal{A}^n} \mathcal{P}(\underline{v}) \mathcal{U}(\underline{v})$$

It should be remarked that the expression for $L_u^{(n)}$ in (3.18) contains an n-th order probability distribution $Q^{(n)}$, i.e. a probability distribution on the elements $\underline{v}$ of $\mathcal{A}^n$:

$$(3.20) \quad L_u^{(n)} = \sum_{\underline{v} \in \mathcal{A}^n} \frac{\mathcal{P}(\underline{v}) \mathcal{U}(\underline{v})}{\sum_{\underline{w} \in \mathcal{A}^n} \mathcal{P}(\underline{w}) \mathcal{U}(\underline{w})} \mathcal{N}(\underline{v}) = \sum_{\underline{v} \in \mathcal{A}^n} Q^{(n)}(\underline{v}) \mathcal{N}(\underline{v})$$

but the sequence $\{Q^{(n)}\}_n$ of these auxiliary probability distributions does not constitute a process, because it does not satisfy the Kolmogorov condition of compatibility. This actually depends on the additive (rather than multiplicative) character of $\mathcal{U}(\underline{v})$. However, in spite of this incompatibility, we shall see that the limiting behaviour of this sequence of probability distributions is such as to permit us interesting conclusions.

Now, referring to the scheme of Fig. 3.1, and assuming that blocks are encoded instead of single letters, one could do the same considerations, and introduce a cost function $c(\underline{v})$ on the blocks, which depends both on $\mathcal{N}(\underline{v})$ and on $\mathcal{U}(\underline{v})$. If one adopts the usual function

$$(3.21) \qquad c(\underline{v}) = \mathcal{N}(\underline{v}) \mathcal{U}(\underline{v})$$

then, for each value of n the user should try to minimize the average cost per source letter, i.e. the quantity

A Lower Bound on $L_u^{(n)}$

$$\frac{1}{n} \sum_{\underline{v} \in \mathcal{A}^n} \mathcal{P}(\underline{v})\mathcal{N}(\underline{v})\mathcal{U}(\underline{v}) ,$$

or equivalently the quantity

$$\frac{1}{n} \frac{\sum_{\underline{v} \in \mathcal{A}^n} \mathcal{P}(\underline{v})\mathcal{N}(\underline{v})\mathcal{U}(\underline{v})}{\sum_{\underline{v} \in \mathcal{A}^n} \mathcal{P}(\underline{v})\mathcal{U}(\underline{v})} , \qquad (3.22)$$

which, by (3.20), is nothing else than

$$\frac{1}{n} L_u^{(n)} . \qquad (3.23)$$

Now, all the considerations made so far for the case $n = 1$ can be repeated and lead to the following results for $n > 1$:

Theorem 3.3

For any value of n, the average useful length of a u.d. code satisfies the following inequality

$$L_u^{(n)} \geq \frac{H^{(n)}(\mathcal{P}, \mathcal{U}) - \overline{u \log u}^{(n)} + \overline{u}^{(n)} \log \overline{u}^{(n)}}{\overline{u}^{(n)} \log m} .$$

Proof.

It is an immediate consequence of Theorem 3.1, provided we consider $\mathcal{Q}^{(n)}$ and $\mathcal{A}^n$ instead of $\mathcal{Q}$ and $\mathcal{A}$.

Q.d.e.

(*) Obviously $\overline{u \log u}^{(n)}$ stands for $\sum_{\underline{v} \in \mathcal{A}^n} \mathcal{P}(\underline{v}) \mathcal{U}(\underline{v}) \log \mathcal{U}(\underline{v})$.

Theorem 3.4

By properly choosing the lengths $\mathcal{N}(\underline{v})$ of the u.d. n-block code, its average useful length $L_u^{(n)}$ can be rendered smaller than

$$(3.24) \qquad \frac{H^{(n)}(\mathcal{P},\mathcal{U}) - \bar{u}\log u + \bar{u}^{(n)}\log\bar{u}^{(n)}}{\bar{u}^{(n)}\log m} + 1$$

Proof

It is sufficient to choose $\mathcal{N}(\underline{v})$ as to satisfy

$$Q^{-\mathcal{N}(\underline{v})} \leq \frac{\mathcal{P}(\underline{v})\mathcal{U}(\underline{v})}{\bar{u}^{(n)}} \leq Q^{-\mathcal{N}(\underline{v})+1} \qquad (\underline{v}\in\mathcal{A}^n)$$

which is always possible, and then one proceeds as usual.

Now, to investigate the asymptotic behaviour of the quantity $\dfrac{L_n^{(n)}}{n}$ as n goes to infinity, we make the following remarks:

i) $\bar{u}^{(n)} = \sum\limits_{\underline{v}\in\mathcal{A}^n}\mathcal{U}(\underline{v})\mathcal{P}(\underline{v}) = \sum\limits_{i_1=1}^{k}\sum\limits_{i_2=1}^{k}\ldots\sum\limits_{i_n=1}^{k}(u_{i_1}+u_{i_2}+\ldots+u_{i_n})p_{i_1}p_{i_2}\ldots p_{i_n} =$

$= \sum\limits_{i_1=1}^{k}p_{i_1}u_{i_1}\sum\limits_{i_2=1}^{k}p_{i_2}\ldots\sum\limits_{i_n=1}^{k}p_{i_n} + \sum\limits_{i_1=1}^{k}p_{i_1}\sum\limits_{i_2=1}^{k}p_{i_2}u_{i_2}\ldots\sum\limits_{i_n=1}^{k}p_{i_n} + \ldots$

$= \sum\limits_{i_1=1}^{k}p_{i_1}u_{i_1} + \sum\limits_{i_2=1}^{k}p_{i_2}u_{i_2} + \ldots + \sum\limits_{i_n=1}^{k}p_{i_n}u_{i_n} = \bar{u} + \bar{u} + \ldots + \bar{u}$

i.e. $\bar{u}^{(n)} = n\bar{u}$

(3.25)

ii) $H^{(n)}(\mathcal{P}, \mathcal{U}) = - \sum_{\underline{v} \in \mathcal{A}^n} \mathcal{U}(\underline{v}) \mathcal{P}(\underline{v}) \log \mathcal{P}(\underline{v}) = - \sum_{i_1=1}^{k} \sum_{i_2=1}^{k} \ldots \sum_{i_n=1}^{k} (u_{i_1} + \ldots + u_{i_n}) \cdot$

$\cdot (p_{i_1} \ldots p_{i_n}) \log (p_{i_1} p_{i_2} \ldots p_{i_n}) =$

$= - \sum_{i_1=1}^{k} u_{i_1} p_{i_1} \log p_{i_1} - \ldots \sum_{i_n=1}^{k} u_{i_n} p_{i_n} \log p_{i_n} - \sum_{i_1=1}^{k} \sum_{i_n=1}^{k} u_{i_1} p_{i_1} p_{i_2} \log p_{i_2} +$

$- \ldots - \sum_{i_{n-1}=1}^{k} \sum_{i_n=1}^{k} u_{i_{n-1}} p_{i_{n-1}}, p_{i_n} \log p_{i_n} = H(\mathcal{P}, \mathcal{U}) + \ldots + H(\mathcal{P}, \mathcal{U}) +$

$+ \bar{u} H(\mathcal{P}) + \ldots + \bar{u} H(\mathcal{P})$

i.e. $H^{(n)}(\mathcal{P}, \mathcal{U}) \equiv n H(\mathcal{P}, \mathcal{U}) + n(n-1) \bar{u} H(\mathcal{P})$

(3.26)

moreover it is possible to upper- and lowerbound the quantity $\overline{u \log u}^{(n)}$; actually

$\overline{u \log u}^{(n)} = \sum_{\underline{v} \in \mathcal{A}^n} \mathcal{P}(\underline{v}) \mathcal{U}(\underline{v}) \log \mathcal{U}(\underline{v}) = \sum_{i_1=1}^{k} \ldots \sum_{i_n=1}^{k} p_{i_1} \ldots p_{i_n} (u_{i_1} + \ldots + u_{i_n}) \cdot$

$\cdot \log (u_{i_1} + \ldots + u_{i_n})$

and if we put

$u^* = \max_{1 \leq i \leq k} u_i$, $u_* = \min_{1 \leq i \leq k} u_i$ (3.27)

also

$$\log n u_* \sum_{i_1=1}^{k} \ldots \sum_{i_n=1}^{k} p_{i_1} \ldots p_{i_n}(u_{i_1}+\ldots+u_{i_n}) \le$$

$$\overline{u \log u}^{(n)} \le \log n \overline{u^*} \sum_{i_1=1}^{k} \ldots \sum_{i_1=1}^{k} p_{i_1} \ldots p_{i_n}(u_{i_1}+\ldots+u_{i_n}) ,$$

whence immediately

(3.28) $\qquad n\bar{u} \log n u_* \le \overline{u \log u}^{(n)} \le n\bar{u} \log n u^* .$

Now we can use expressions (3.25) and (3.26) as well as inequalities (3.28) for deriving the bounds expressed by the following Lemma:

<u>Lemma 3.1</u>

There exists a sequence of block codes for the considered memoryless source having utilities for which the ratio $\dfrac{L_u^{(n)}}{n}$ satisfies the following inequalities:

$$\frac{nH(\mathcal{P},\mathcal{U}) + n(n-1)H(\mathcal{P})\bar{u} - n\bar{u}\log nu^* + n\bar{u}\log n\bar{u}}{n^2 \bar{u} \log m} \le \frac{L_u^{(n)}}{n} <$$

$$< \frac{nH(\mathcal{P},\mathcal{U}) + n(n-1)H(\mathcal{P})\bar{u} - n\bar{u}\log nu_* + n\bar{u}\log n\bar{u}}{n^2 \bar{u} \log m} + \frac{1}{n} .$$

(3.29)

The inequalities in (3.29) can be better grasped if one put

(3.30) $\qquad B_1 = \left(\dfrac{H(\mathcal{P},\mathcal{U})}{\bar{u}} - H(\mathcal{P}) + \log \dfrac{\bar{u}}{u^*} \right) \log m ,$

$$B_2 = \left(\frac{H(\mathcal{P},\mathcal{U})}{\bar{u}} - H(\mathcal{P}) + \log \frac{\bar{u}}{u_*} \right) \frac{1}{\log m} + 1 . \qquad (3.31)$$

Then $\dfrac{L_u^{(n)}}{n}$ is upper and lower bounded as follows:

$$H(\mathcal{P}) + \frac{1}{n} B_1 \le \frac{L_u^{(n)}}{n} < H(\mathcal{P}) + \frac{1}{n} B_2 . \qquad (3.32)$$

One additional element for studying the asymptotic behaviour of $\dfrac{L_u^{(n)}}{n}$ is provided by the following

Lemma 3.2

The constants B_1 and B_2 defined by (3.30) and (3.31) satisfy the following inequalities:

$$B_1 \le 0 \qquad (3.33)$$

$$B_2 \ge 1 \qquad (3.34)$$

where the equality signs hold iff the utilities u_i are all equal.

Proof

We shall prove that $B_1 \le 0$; the proof of (3.34) is quite similar. Since, apart from the positive factor

$$\frac{1}{\log m} , \quad B_1 = \sum_1^k \frac{p_i u_i}{\bar{u}} \log \frac{1}{p_i} - \sum_1^k p_i \log \frac{1}{p_i} + \log \frac{\bar{u}}{u^*} ,$$

putting

$$\frac{u_i}{u^*} = s_i$$

one gets

$$B_1 = \sum_i^k \left(p_i \frac{s_i}{\bar{s}} - p_i\right) \log \frac{1}{p_i} + \log \bar{s} \le \sum_i^k p_i \left(\frac{s_i}{\bar{s}} - 1\right) \log \frac{1}{p_i} \quad (\text{actually } \bar{s} \le 1),$$

and consequently

$$B_1 < \log \frac{1}{p_*} \sum_i^k p_i \left(\frac{s_i}{\bar{s}} - 1\right) = 0 \;,$$

where $p_* = \min_{1 \le i \le k} p_i$.

Of course if $u_i = \text{const.}$, then $B_1 = 0$.

After these preparations the following theorem follows immediately:

Theorem 3.5

Given a discrete (finite) memoryless source having utilities, there exists a sequence of u.d. block codes whose average useful length per source letter tends to the Shannon entropy $H(\mathcal{G})$ of the source.

Proof.

It is sufficient to let n go to infinity in (3.32).

Q.d.e.

From Lemma 3.2 one sees immediately that for each value of n the ratio $L_u^{(n)}/n$ lies within a region like that shown in Fig. 3.2

Asymptotic Behaviour of $L_u^{(n)}/n$

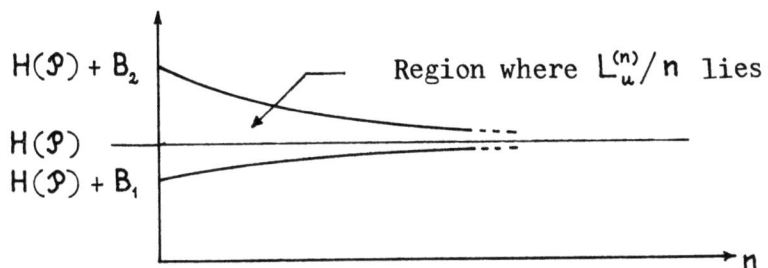

Fig. 3.2 Illustrating the behaviour of $L_u^{(n)}/n$.

It is not clear, however, whether $\dfrac{L_u^{(n)}}{n}$ tends to $H(\mathcal{P})$ from above, from below or in a somewhat oscillating way. This point seems to be important, since it gives indications as to whether the block length should be made very large or not.

There is a general consideration concerning this point. On one hand, if n is very large, the further flexibility in coding provided by the presence of the utilities disappears, since their influence dies off as indicated by Theorem 3.5. On the other hand, if n is very small one can suspect that there are rather large losses, due to the inefficiency of single-letter coding, as in the classical case. Therefore one could feel that there is an intermediate " optimal " length for the blocks, at which the function $L_u^{(n)}/n$ has a minimum value.

Following this reasoning the $\dfrac{L_u^{(n)}}{n}$ curve should be as depicted in Fig. 3.3.

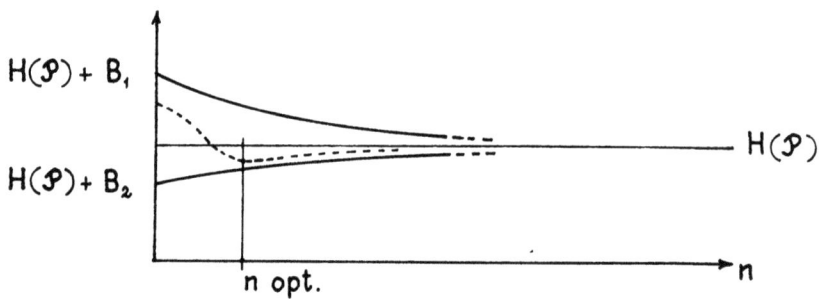

Fig. 3.3 One possible behaviour of $L_u^{(n)}/n$.

Of course this does not exclude that the optimal value for n be 1.

There is however another, more precise, reasoning concerning this point. Consider primary blocks of length mn and use the same n-block code for each of the m subblocks. We wish to investigate on the sign of the following difference

$$(3.35) \qquad \frac{L_u^{(mn)}}{mn} - \frac{L_u^{(n)}}{n} .$$

It is not difficult to see that

$$(3.36) \qquad \frac{L_u^{(mn)}}{mn} - \frac{L_u^{(n)}}{n} = \frac{1}{n} \frac{m-1}{m} \{L^{(n)} - L_u^{(n)}\} ,$$

where $L_u^{(n)}$ is the n-th order average useful length; and $L^{(n)}$ is the n-th order normal average length:

$$L^{(n)} = \sum_{\underline{v} \in \mathcal{A}^n} \mathcal{N}(\underline{v}) \mathcal{P}(\underline{v}) .$$

Therefore the sign of the difference appearing in (3.35) is the same as of the difference

$$L^{(n)} - L_u^{(n)} = \sum_{\underline{v} \in A^n} \mathcal{P}(\underline{v}) \mathcal{N}(\underline{v}) \left\{ 1 - \frac{\mathcal{U}(\underline{v})}{\bar{\mathcal{U}}^{(n)}} \right\}. \qquad (3.37)$$

In particular, for $n = 1$, the difference (3.35) becomes

$$\frac{L_u^{(m)}}{m} - L_u = \left(1 - \frac{1}{m}\right) \sum_i^k p_i \, l_i \left(1 - \frac{u_i}{\bar{u}}\right), \qquad (3.38)$$

being as usual l_i the codeword length for letter a_i. So the behaviour of $\frac{L_u^{(m)}}{n}$ depends on the mean value of the random variable $\mathcal{N}(\underline{v}) \left\{ 1 - \frac{\mathcal{U}(\underline{v})}{\bar{\mathcal{U}}^{(n)}} \right\}$ or in particular of the random variable $l_i \left(1 - \frac{u_i}{\bar{u}}\right)$. Since the random variable $1 - \frac{\mathcal{U}(\underline{v})}{\bar{\mathcal{U}}^{(n)}}$ has zero mean, to obtain e.g. a negative sign, for the difference (3.35) one should associate large values of $\mathcal{N}(\underline{v})$ to the sequence $\underline{v}$ for which $\mathcal{U}(\underline{v})$ is large.

Obviously this association can lead to a negative sign of the difference (3.35), i.e. to a decreasing character of the function $L_u^{(n)}/n$, only provided the limitations expressed by inequalities (3.32) are satisfied. This means that after a decreasing behaviour, the curve may exhibit an increasing behaviour to comply with (3.32)..

It is to be remarked that the function $L_u^{(n)}/n$ is not uniquely defined once and for all, since there is one for each possible sequence of u.d. codes. Here we refer to the "best" function, i.e. to that having the smallest value for each value of n. On the other hand the best function corresponds to the choice $m^{-\mathcal{N}(\underline{v})} \leq Q^{(n)}(\underline{v}) \leq m^{-\mathcal{N}(\underline{v})+1}$ for each value of n.

To end up with this chapter, let us point out that if we adopt the additive definition for the utility of a sequence $\underline{v} = v_1 \ldots v_n$ of independent and equally distributed random variables, say:

$$u(\underline{v}) = u(v_1) + u(v_2) + \ldots + u(v_n)$$

then the ratio $\dfrac{u(\underline{v})}{n}$ by the weak law of the large numbers tends in probability to the common mean value of the random variables $u(v_i)$, which we have designated by $\bar{u}$ ($\bar{u} = \sum_{1}^{k} p_i u_i$):

(3.39) $$\lim_{n \to \infty} \text{prob.} \frac{u(\underline{v})}{n} = \bar{u} .$$

On the other hand, the statistical structure of the memoryless source implies that the emitted sequences are "typical" with probability tending to 1 (cf. G. Longo (1970)), where by typical sequence we mean one whose probability is approximately $\mathcal{P}(\underline{v}) \cong 2^{-nH(\mathcal{P})}$:

(3.40) $$\lim_{n \to \infty} \text{prob.} \, \mathcal{P}(\underline{v}) = 2^{-nH(\mathcal{P})} .$$

From (3.39) and (3.40) we can conclude that

(3.41) $$\lim_{n \to \infty} \text{prob.} \frac{\mathcal{N}(\underline{v})}{n} = H(\mathcal{P}) ,$$

because the best for $\mathcal{N}(\underline{v})$ is $m^{-\mathcal{N}(\underline{v})} \cong \dfrac{\mathcal{P}(\underline{v}) u(\underline{v})}{n \bar{u}}$.

Expression (3.41) is an alternative proof, though weaker, of Theorem 3.5, since the codeword lengths $\mathcal{N}(\underline{v})$ were chosen to minimize the average useful length per source letter $\dfrac{L_u^{(n)}}{n}$ and not the average length per source letter $\frac{L^{(n)}}{n}$. As a consequence, the transmission cost $\frac{\mathcal{N}(\underline{v})\,\mathcal{U}(\underline{v})}{n\,\bar{u}}$ for an n-tuple $\underline{v}$ is given by $\mathcal{N}(\underline{v})$, and therefore with a probability approaching 1 in the limit, by $n\,H(\mathcal{P})$. The average cost is therefore $H(\mathcal{P})$, as stated by Theorem 3.5.

This result, that the presence of the utilities has no relevance when n goes to infinity, and that only the probability distribution plays a role, is obviously a consequence of the definition the utility of a sequence. On the other hand such a definition seems quite reasonable for memoryless sources.

Conclusions

As we have seen, there seems to be a need for the completion of the Information concept by means of some " subjective ", non statistical, element. Such an element could perhaps be the utility, which we have dealt with in these notes.

On the other hand, although interesting in its own, the utility concept, as we have formalized it does not seem to enter deeply in the coding procedures. Either one should introduce the utilities in a different way, or the theorem in which utility is relevant are not yet known; whatever the situation may be, the impression is that the philosophical importance of the utility concept should be reflected more deeply in the formalization.

Moreover it seems difficult to extend the utility considerations to include information channels besides information sources. The attempts made so far to find a relationship with the theory of Cost Scales have failed, probably on account of an intrinsic difference between the two concepts.

References

[1] Belis M., Guiaşu S. (1968) " A Quantitative - Qualitative Measure of Information etc." IEEE Trans. Inform. Theory, IT-14, 1968, p. 593-594.

[2] Csiszár I., Katona G.O.H., Tusnády G.O.H. (1969) " Information Sources with Different Cost Scales and the Principle of Conservation of Entropy" Z. Wahrsch. U. Verw. Geb. 12 (1969), 185-222.

[3] Gallager R.G. (1968) " Information Theory and Reliable Communication" J. Wiley & Sons, 1968.

[4] Guiaşu S. (1971) " Weigthed Entropy" Rep. on Mathematical Physics, vol. 2, pp. 165-179, 1971.

[5] Guiaşu S., Picard C.F. (1971) " Borne inférieure de la longueur utile de certains codes" C.R. Acad. Sc. Paris, t. 273 (26 Juillet 1971).

[6] Katona G.O.H. (1970) " General Theory of Noiseless Channels" CISM Courses and Lectures N° 31, Udine, 1970.

[7] Katona G.O.H., Tusnády G.O.H. (1967) " The Principle of Conservation of Entropy in a Noiseless Channel" Studia Sci. Hungar. 2, 29 - 35.

[8] Longo G. (1970) " Source Coding Theory" CISM Course and Lectures N°32, Udine, 1970

[9] Shannon C.E. & Weaver (1949) " The Mathematical Theory of Communication" The University of Illinois Press, Urbana, 1949.

Contents

	Page
Preface..	3
Chapter 1 : Fundamentals About Coding for Noiseless Channels..................................	5
Chapter 2 : The Communication Problem: the Statistical, the Semantic and the Effectiveness Viewpoints - Sources Having Utilities and the Useful Entropy.......................	17
Chapter 3 : Some Coding Problems and Theorems Relative to Sources Having a Utility Distribution	27
Conclusions...	47
References..	49
Contents..	50

MIX
Papier aus verantwortungsvollen Quellen
Paper from responsible sources
FSC® C105338

If you have any concerns about our products,
you can contact us on
ProductSafety@springernature.com

In case Publisher is established outside the EU,
the EU authorized representative is:
**Springer Nature Customer Service Center GmbH
Europaplatz 3, 69115 Heidelberg, Germany**

Printed by Libri Plureos GmbH
in Hamburg, Germany